FINDING FREEDOM IN FEARLESS GROWTH®

(Book 2)

Learn to run your race with confidence, courage, without apology, and with…

NO FEAR

Becky Michel

NO FEAR: FINDING FREEDOM IN FEARLESS GROWTH®

Cover design by Becky Michel

Printed in the United States of America

ISBN #978-1-68489-616-5

NO FEAR – Finding freedom in Fearless Growth®–book two of three. We will learn about fear and ourselves. How to get honest about who we are and the essential things to experiencing our best life. Intentional change is necessary to experience true growth. Take a journey with me as we dig into Fearless Growth® with NO FEAR!

Fearless Growth Leader and Expert
Becky Michel
CE publishing

About Becky

Fearless Growth Expert – Becky Michel is the Author & Creator of Fearless Growth®. She has applied and shared this process for over a decade.

Author – of the three-part Fearless Growth® series as well as a series of children's self-help books. All publications are from a faith-based perspective. Fearless Growth® is a lifelong process. It is a journey to become exactly who God created you to be. God gave Becky Fearless Growth® to begin changing herself and then to help others. Change, choice, and challenge abound at the core of living a Fearless Growth® life. You must want to change your beliefs, actions, and mindset.

Speaker – Becky brings an inspiring message of becoming the person God created you to be by standing up for yourself throughout that renovation process–Fearless Growth®. She shows you how to live life on purpose and push through the challenges that hold you back from experiencing growth and freedom in Christ so you can live free from addictions, childhood grievances, and the daily struggles of life.

Coach – Becky offers a Fearless Growth® coaching program that is "Real Life" constructed. It is about being honest with yourself about who and where you are. You will begin the process of change today, yet you will not do it alone! Let Becky help you discover–Fearless Growth®!

Creative Expressions is a division of Becky Michel.

For booking or more information, contact Becky at:

BeckyMichel.com

417-293-5340

Becky@BeckyMichel.com

Table of Contents

Foreword 1

Introduction..5

Chapter 1: Change 7

Chapter 2: It's Okay To Chase Your Dream 17

Chapter 3: Who Am I? 25

Chapter 4: Fearless Growth® 33

Chapter 5: Facing Giants With Love..37

Chapter 6: Courage With Heart 41

Chapter 7: The Process Of Fearless Growth® Realness......................49

Chapter 8: No Limits 55

Chapter 9: Perspective...61

Chapter 10: The Right Time 67

Chapter 11: Failing Forward 71

Chapter 12: Stand 75

Chapter 13: Unashamed 81

References: Check out my other books and resources 86

Bonus Section:...89

Foreword

I have watched Becky move from fearful to fearless over the last few years and it has been such a beautiful journey to watch. She knows a thing or two about pushing past your fears and growing your faith, confidence and courage.

Finding Freedom in Fearless Growth walks you through the principles needed in order to live beyond your fears and stretch beyond your comfort zone so you can design a life you love. Staying in your comfort zone will kill your dreams. This book shows you how to become more courageous and confident. You'll find strategies to help you become more brave and bold.

You don't have to just wish you were bolder, you can be bolder and live with no fear. There is a fearless person lurking inside of you! Are you ready to meet that version of yourself?

We live in a world with many threats, challenges and problems. All giving us a reason to be fearful. The world needs this message and as the Fearless Growth Expert, Becky's voice is refreshing and inspiring.

Her message will help you stop worrying about what others will think of you. You'll be inspired to answer questions such as , "What am I really afraid of?" and "What's the worst that can happen?"

She provides powerful tactics so you know what to do when you're feeling fearful and how to deal with stressors that lead to fear. When you follow the strategies provided in *Finding Freedom in Fearless Growth*, your will become prepared to confront your negative and fearful thoughts and reprogram yourself to replace them with new positive thought and actions. Plus, you'll develop the skill and confidence needed to overcome your fears so you can walk in freedom.

The best way to overcome a fear reaction is to relax. You can train yourself to automatically relax when you first feel fear. This book teaches you how to trust God to help you through your challenges so you can begin to relax knowing you are not dealing with the stressors and fear alone. Becky beautifully shares her faith and models for us how to walk in faith over fear.

I too have had to learn how to press forward in spite of my fears. One of my greatest weapons is the reality that many of the things I feared never actually came true! Some studies suggest the number of things we fear that actually come true is less than 20%. So, there's an 80% chance your fears won't come true. If you can deal with the worst possible outcome, and there's only a 20% chance it will even happen, you have little to worry about.

I am an international speaker and digital marketing expert. I've traveled the world helping people build magnetic and influential personal brands. I've even been given the honor of being ranked #8 among the top 30 brand gurus in the world. Having shared that, you would think that I never deal with fear.

I wish that were true!
I believe that dealing with fear is an ongoing battle that requires you to be intentional everyday about trusting God, strengthening your faith, becoming more courage and building your confidence. Realize that fear only happens between your ears. Almost all fears are unique. You might be afraid of snakes, but your friend isn't. You might be afraid of heights, but your sister finds them exhilarating. In most instances, you are the source of your fear.

This book will help you focus on the positive possibilities rather than thinking about every little thing that might go wrong. It will encourage you to focus instead on what might go right. Allow yourself to feel excited about the possibilities.

Learn to view fear as a challenge. Think of fear as the beginning of a game. See if you can get yourself to take an action that makes you afraid when you think about doing something you fear.

You can live a fearless life and experience many more rewarding adventures when you accept that your fears are manufactured inside your head.

I want you to know that you can let them go and be bold.

Start today by doing something you've always wanted to do but didn't quite have enough courage. Just relax and do it. Show yourself that there's nothing to fear.

Imagine how much more exciting your life would be if you give yourself the chance to have something amazing happen each day!

Lethia Owens, CSP
Game Changers International, LLC
Founder of Faith Fueled Life and Women of Audacious Faith
www.LethiaOwens.com

Introduction

Fear—what does it mean to you? Fear is not one of my favorite subjects! I mean, who enjoys talking about the things in life we dread discussing or try to avoid? I don't particularly like the subject, as it's not at all pleasant. However, I do believe fear is the number one thing that keeps us stuck. It holds us back from being the best version of ourselves. It holds us back from who God has created us to be.

Experiencing Fearless Growth® doesn't mean you never have fears. It's a guide to help you recognize, overcome and push through when fear does rear its ugly head.

God doesn't want us to camp out on the circumstances out of our control that keep us from moving forward or prevent us from pushing through life's many issues. You can achieve your very best growth when you recognize those unlovely places or challenges in your life— then addressing them in the way, He wants you to. Each person's journey is unique. This begins the process of Fearless Growth®.

God gave me the process of Fearless Growth® over ten years to grow me into who He has called me to be. Through the Fearless Growth® process, you'll realize your true identity, discover your purpose, and live your best life that God designed for you.

This book is part of a three-part series. It's an overview of my Fearless Growth® journey and is my story of personal struggles & thoughts. It's how God brought me to that exact place where I now have the privilege of helping others discover Fearless Growth® by making changes to their beliefs, actions, and mindsets.

So again, welcome, now let's get growing.

CHAPTER 1
change

"Those that mind don't matter,

and those who matter don't mind."

– Dr. Seuss

For God hath not given us the spirit of fear; but of power, and of love, and of a sound mind (2 Timothy 1:7).

Fearless Growth® is about learning to break the chains of fear that keep you in bondage and hold you back. It teaches you how to stop allowing the enemy to have his way with you. When you become aware of his fear tactics and learn to overcome that fear, you'll understand the freedom that comes from power, love, and a sound mind.

I woke up at 4:00 am one November morning with that verse resounding in my heart. It was God prompting me that it's time to start my Fearless Growth® journey.

This verse convinces us, from the beginning, that no matter what we go through in life, no matter how big the giants we face, our God has already made away. It reminds us, when others make us feel intimidated or insecure, we can stand with boldness, confidence, courage, and the heart to face our challenges.

What a statement of His love, strength, and peace all in one verse! He loves us enough to equip us so we can endure the hard times, the struggles, and the negativity of this world. He strengthens us so we can push through the bad times and challenging relationships. He empowers us to get up and keep going no matter what.

So, this scripture reminds you that you can move forward with courage and boldness. You're stronger than you think and braver than you believe even in those moments of weakness and most of all…

-You are enough and greatly loved!-

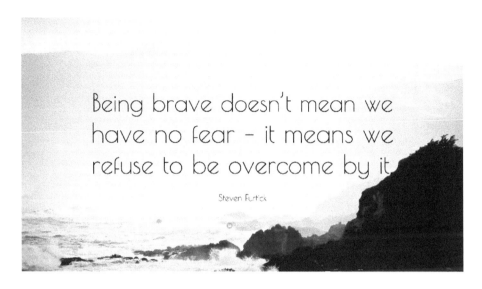

Being brave doesn't mean we have no fear – it means we refuse to be overcome by it

Steven Furtick

When we reflect on our lives, there's always a positive and a negative aspect. Think about it. Have you ever had a pity party about your childhood? Perhaps, your birth order, you felt like the black sheep, your parents didn't show you love as a kid or maybe even an adult?

Do you believe everything you remember is true, or is it possible the enemy is planting seeds of doubt and fear so that you view it with a negative perspective? Maybe, growing up, you had no choice but to think what you thought and feel what you felt.

What if you could have seen your birth order as a blessing? What if you saw being the black sheep as a gift? What if feeling a lack of love was an opportunity to draw closer to God and project more love yourself?

As we go through life, we experience both good and bad moments and good and bad feelings. No matter the circumstance, you have two choices, two outcomes and two ways to see it. It's the one we choose to see that determines our mood, mindset, attitude, and next steps in life.

Have you ever experienced a negative outcome from making a wrong choice? If you're like me, that's an understatement.

Why do we do what we know is wrong, over and over? Like Paul said: "For the good that I would I do not: but the evil which I would not, that I do (Romans 7:19)."

Have you ever experienced a Jesus *whipping*? If so, you'll understand when I say, "how can someone so smart be so careless?" I think that's a pleasant way of putting it.

Unfortunately, we repeatedly find ourselves in these exact situations. This baffling disobedience has been happening since the beginning of time.

Yep, from the beginning of time, starting with Eve – thanks woman– continuing through today. When we examine people in the Bible, we see Jacob was a cheater; Peter had a temper, David had an affair, Noah got drunk and naked, the woman at the well had five husbands and wasn't married to the sixth one. Let's not forget; Jonah ran from God; Paul was a murderer. The list goes on.

God shows us repeatedly throughout His Word that He loves to take the most broken, problemed people and turn their lives around. He pulls them out of the pit for His perfect purpose and gives them a second, third and tenth chance. He's done the same for me! How many times has God thrown me a lifeline over the years? An unbelievable amount! How about you?

So, let's define Fearless Growth®.

Fearless Growth® is the process of personal growth from a biblical perspective. A way to experience realness through understanding who you are and the unmeasurable value you have in Christ. This understanding allows you to fulfill the unique calling of being you. You'll also have the strength to live a life of freedom, boldness, love, peace, and sincerity. You'll no longer worry about what others might think.

As you learn the characteristics of this type of growth and begin applying the principles, you'll activate Fearless Growth®.

You can't fulfill your dreams without the skills to think, feel and become the genuine version of yourself. When you experience the freedom to have authentic realness, you can be more, do more, dream more, and accomplish more. No matter your age.

God's desire for you is deliverance. Deliverance comes when you have the freedom to become your best self and live the life you were born to live. Anyone, anywhere, at any time, can make changes, grow, and experience deliverance.

I'm not the same person I was five minutes ago. Just like me, you can change at any time. No one is stopping you—but you.

To have Fearless Growth® we must be willing to admit our mental state. Next, we must desire to change and be courageous enough to do so.

Let's talk about our mental state. Our mental state can affect us far more than we realize. When I say the mental state, I am referring to our state of mind. This state includes our emotions, physical body, feelings, thoughts, and energy. These are all elements that God created us with that affect our brains.

While I'm not going to dive into every aspect of how the mind works, I'm going to say that it's vital to grasp the seriousness of self-care, especially if you've gone through a tragedy or you're sad, angry, or fearful.

Webster dictionary depicts mental state this way: our body is in a sound state or a weak state or has recovered from a feeble state. Example: The state of his health is good, or the state of his mind is favorable for study.

Your mental state is the condition that you're in at a specific time. Anything can affect your mental state, including your environment. Is it fast-paced or loud? Do you love it or hate it? Are you working a job you're terrible at? How about experiencing uncomfortable situations, fighting, politics, etc.? Even the monotony of your daily chores and tasks can affect your mental state.

Maybe you're in a miserable place where you'd rather scrub a thousand toilets than be there one more day. I've been there, working a job I couldn't stand, being around someone that never changes or desires to change their needy, pitiful, woes-is-me state. These conditions affect our state, and we may not even realize the full impact.

Let me ask you, do you have a filter set up? Are you aware of what you allow into your mind? More so, what do you allow to stay? This filter applies to your mind, home, relationship with God and others. It also includes your body, energy, and life.

Take a moment, to be honest about your present mental state by answering the following questions. These questions will help you in continuing the Fearless Growth® process.

- How do I handle stress?

- How do I process unhappiness?

- How do I tackle problems?

- How do I express my frustrations?

- How do I deal with people?

- Am I happy with who I am?

- Am I ready and willing to make changes that bring Fearless Growth®?

- As a child of God, do I have a desire to grow in the direction He wants me to–even if it might feel uncomfortable?

- What would I change if I had the opportunity? It could be something external like your circumstances or internal like a characteristic, trait, or habit.

- Picture my life five years from now. Are the actions I'm taking now moving me closer to that picture or further away?

- Can I be honest with myself about want I need to change in my life? That can be anything from actions I take, foods I eat, places I go, people I hang with, etc.

- Am I aware of my mental state?

- Is my mental state good, excellent, or poor? Rate it!

Mental health is a fundamental matter that needs to be adequately addressed.

- Stop and assess: do I seem more down than up, feel bad more than good, foggy in the head, or find myself full of negative self-talk and energy each day? Maybe I have trouble hearing or understanding someone?

Sometimes it's a simple fix, like a good vitamin supplement, more sleep, getting your teeth cleaned, joining a gym, or even getting a hearing aid. These minor fixes can make all the difference between being in an excellent state or an okay state.

- Do I have any more significant concerns I should address? Perhaps therapy, counseling, coaching, scheduling a doctor's visit, hiring a house cleaner, checking into a rehab center, etc. Answer yes or no.

- If yes, describe my concerns:

As you read, you may notice I repeat myself. God has spent a lot of time repeating things to me in my life. It was a key to helping me grasp what He was trying to teach me. I believe it'll help you too.

You must be willing to surrender the struggles that hold you back. We have the power to transform ourselves and our lives. However, until we genuinely want it, it won't happen. Just like anything else you do in life, without being aware of what you need, making it a priority, and setting goals, you'll never experience the process of a personal growth journey–a Fearless Growth® journey.

Through this Fearless Growth® journey, God has taught me to be ME! Not the version others intended for my life, but who He created me to be through changing my beliefs, actions, and mindset. God has also taught me to be patient, have faith, stand up for myself, and run my race.

I pray that as I share pieces of my life, including my struggles, blessings, and self-discovery, it gives you the courage to start your Fearless Growth® journey.

it's okay to chase your dream

"When you learn the value in your identity, you'll never compromise your values again because God is no respecter of persons."

– Becky Michel

How the world often perceives your dream depends on your circle of influence. I hope you have nothing but encouragers and kindhearted people in your corner, yet that's not always the case. It's interesting how we can quickly compromise or accept someone else's judgment or opinion towards our dream or vision.

Do you get angry, get even, or get sad towards those critical people? If you said yes to any of those questions, I think there's some room for growth, my friend.

When God gave me a vision, it changed my life! When you have a clear grasp on your identity, you're empowered to let go of their opinions. You can walk away when others cast judgment, fling disapproving words, or condemn you. I'm continually letting go of this judgment.

How do you believe God sees you? Who are you in His eyes? What has He revealed to you about your unique self? What's inside you? Personality, character, likes, dislikes, interests, abilities, gifts?

Has God deposited something specific that burns in your heart? Has He birthed a vision or dream inside you?

Whether our dreams are private or public, big or small, we need faith to move them forward. Faith is the one thing we must practice so we can accomplish anything God calls us to do.

Faith is the substance of things hoped for, the evidence of things not seen (Hebrews 11:1).

Embracing a dream or calling that God put in your heart is a humbling experience. If you had a dream once but never allowed God to fulfill it, I encourage you to take it back out and talk to Him about it.

Like me, you may have pondered the dream or questioned it. Possibly, you've attempted a test run and got some negative feedback. Perhaps, it knocked you down–more than once–and, most likely, you struggled to get back up again.

The great news is Fearless Growth® equips you to face your fears, so you're free to pursue your ideas, dreams, and visions courageously.

Let me ask you this–do you know your "why"?

Ten years ago, God showed me the importance of discovering my "why."

God instructs us to occupy until He comes. Don't wander without a plan, purpose, or goals. God created you for great things. You're His unique creation–His masterpiece. Realize that you would not be here if He didn't want you to be.

God gave me a vision years ago–a dream. This vision revealed to me who I am and who God created me to be. Yet, when I looked at the gap between who I was and who God created me to be, sadly, the two were a far cry from one another.

God gave me a heart for people. Not just any people, but hurting people, like me and like you. Let's be real for a second; if you're a living, breathing human being, someone hurt you.

God showed me how I had always allowed the opinion of others to guide everything I did, from my parenting to my convictions, to my conversation, to my language. It affected my hobbies and my abilities. The value I placed on other's opinions infiltrated my very existence and formed my belief system. Now that's some excessive people-pleasing, people!

After experiencing all that, He implored me to share what I learned with others!

That means you. Yes, you–you're not reading this by accident!

God's ways are higher than our ways. Many times, we can't comprehend what is happening to us or even why it's happening.

However, Romans 8:28 assures us that all these things are working together for good. We can take comfort in those words.

If I knew then what I know now, I wouldn't be who I am and where I am today. And, you know what? There's no one else I'd rather be.

If you could be anyone in the world right now, who would you be?

Hopefully, you said yourself. Why? Only you know why you think, act, and choose as you do.

We get into trouble when we choose to justify and not take ownership of who we are. When we do this, we believe it's our circumstances that create who we are.

Life is not all rainbows and sunshine. It's a mix of good and bad, both positive and negative. Whether we like to admit it or not, the problem still exists, waiting for you to deal with it, which, by the way, is a choice.

God gave you the power of choice. The question is, are you willing to choose to deal with the situation that needs changing or significant obstacles that need tackling?

If a tree falls in the woods and no one is there to hear it, does it still make a sound? Did it still happen?

Picture this. On one of your many strolls through your favorite woods, you find a giant tree blocking the road.

How did it happen? Did someone cut it down the day before? Maybe the wind blew it over? Perhaps it has an unknown root issue that caused it to fall?

Now what? Do you remove the tree? Do you turn around and leave the woods? Do you try to walk around the tree? Do you call for help?

Imagine for a moment; these woods are a picture of your life. It's where you live, work, and grow.

The fallen tree is a problem or adverse circumstance. It could be an addiction, a stronghold, or a troubled relationship. It's an issue you need to deal with in your life.

When you encountered the tree, aka problem, it might have caught you by surprise. It's also possible you saw the cracks in the truck before, and you chose to ignore it, hoping it was no big deal or would fix itself.

Once you're aware of the issue, it's up to you what you choose to do with it. You could choose to ignore it, or you could choose to acknowledge it. It's up to you.

You can choose to ignore the issue you need to address (that's the tree lying in the road). Going the ostrich route will keep you stuck in a "crazy cycle," continually dealing with the situation. However, if you choose to acknowledge the problem (the fallen tree in the road) and take the necessary steps to improve, you may not have to leave the woods entirely. You might only have to move over a bit. Through all this, you also will defiantly need to do some pruning. All things work out when you deal with the situation (Romans 8:28). A caveat, it just might not work out the way you think it will, yet it will be for the best.

Regardless of how the problem got there, it's now up to you to deal with it. Don't be concerned with how it happened or how you got there because that is in the past. It's more about why and what you're willing to do about it?

If you try any other way, such as going around or over the problem, you'll never have peace and freedom. Yet, once the tree, or issue, is cleared from the road, it not only benefits you but also aids anyone else who comes along that same path.

Acknowledging the problem is the easiest way to fix it, yet it's hard to do, and the hard thing and the right thing are usually the same.

It has felt like a never-ending encounter of coming to know myself, realizing where I was, who I was, and how I got there and then being willing to change–this was where my story began.

Growth can only come by change. You can only make changes by being real about the challenging issues and surrendering the struggles we battle. Accepting those messy and uncomfortable pieces is the only way to begin this process. Are you willing to go there?

If you keep doing what you're doing, I know for sure that you'll keep getting what you're getting. It's up to you to decide whether you get the good, the bad, or the change worthy.

When I was 30, and began changing the areas and things I didn't love about myself and life, I rewound my past. While I promote not living in the past, it is necessary to visit how we got where we are in order to stop unhealthy patterns and make changes for future growth. As I examined myself, I realized several of the people in my life had been making me feel bad, guilty, and dumb for over 15 years. These toxic behaviors would bring a repeat of various fears attached to shaming, guilting, and taking advantage of me. I wish I had known what to look for and how to stop this at an early age, which is why I do what I do today. These struggles would hold me back, as I attempted to do and to be as each person needed me to. It was about what they needed from me in order to feel better about themselves, justify behaviors, or seek approval for their actions, amongst other things I will probably never understand. If I performed according to how someone else needed, only then was I worthy of their attention, affection, and love. They based this type of love on selfish, ulterior motives, expectations, and performance regulations. Is this unconditional love? Unconditional love does not set rules and restrictions in order to be loved. Unconditional love says I love YOU, that's it. Respect is a two-way street that should exist in every relationship and involves laying down our fleshly desires in order to just love another person for who and where they are. Respect does not demand that I do as you say, or submit to things that go against my values. When I was finally able to see how I had allowed others to take advantage of me, and that my efforts were mostly to please others, I became aware enough to stop the actions that took me into those relationships. Sometimes this process can take quite a long time, as we don't get into this snare overnight. It is both a process in and out. If I continue to allow Sally to disrespect me and never stand up to her, she will continue to do it, becoming more and more comfortable doing so as time goes by. However, setting a boundary early in the relationship that stops that behavior will either be a turn off to Sally and she will move on, or it will set the stage for a healthy relationship of which you will both enjoy. When I don't take care of the behaviors that don't feel good to me, I will forever remain in bondage to the person subjecting me to them and it will be very unlikely they change that behavior since I already allowed it. I have personally experienced this where it took years for the changes to happen, and some never did which led to setting strict boundaries and even cutting ties with those who were unwilling to respect me as a human. Again, it's a matter of stopping what we are doing in order to create healthier outcomes. I must change something I am doing in order to alter an unhealthy relationship. Even people we love can take advantage of us, both intentionally and unintentionally, as has happened to me in my life. Some of the unhealthy actions I have experienced from other and done myself are unsatisfied questioning, manipulation, anger, lying, arrogance, blaming, holding grudges, judging, disregarding someone's feelings, people pleasing, and punishment with little things such as not stopping by or giving them the cold shoulder when they do not perform as we need. This is not okay. This is toxic behavior of which you should not be partaking in, either by being the one doing it, or receiving it. The way we fix this is by setting boundaries.

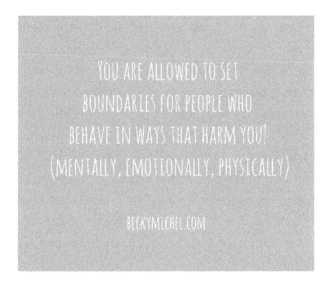

YOU ARE ALLOWED TO SET
BOUNDARIES FOR PEOPLE WHO
BEHAVE IN WAYS THAT HARM YOU!
(MENTALLY, EMOTIONALLY, PHYSICALLY)

BECKYMICHEL.COM

1.   Do you set boundaries?

2.   If not, why?

3.   Are you willing to change this? If not, why?

4.   Do you have any relationships that need boundaries set?

List three things you want to change that will improve your state of being. Examples: consider other's feelings more often, be swifter to hear and slower to speak, not get as angry, be more helpful, stop eating as much sugar, put on a smile each day, develop stronger convictions and values etc. Things to help you move into a healthier space. You get the idea!

1.

2.

3.

CHAPTER 3
who am I?

"People don't care how much you know
until they know how much you care."

– Theodore Roosevelt

If you have problems in your life, **don't** assume there is something wrong with you.

· B R U C E C. H A F E N

BECKYMICHEL.COM

I'm from a small town in South Central, Missouri. Growing up, I always felt like the kid with broken roots, you know, divorced parents, a different home life, the feeling that nobody ever got me—or even gave a crap. Yes, those were lies from the enemy convincing me something was wrong with me from a very young age.

God cares for you much more than you could ever imagine. His love for you is so magnificent there is nothing you can do to change it. You can, however, choose to reject Him. If I can, I want to encourage you not to reject God's unwavering love. No matter where you are, He loves you right now, today, the same as He always has, and He has a plan for you no matter your past.

Unfortunately, as humans, particularly tiny humans, we often don't look to God for that much-needed love. We base our beliefs on the words, actions, or inactions of the adults around us. I've even watched my children experience this when I let them down.

My school experience was a place of familiarity and comfort. As far as learning goes, my education was nothing to write home about. I say that with kindness. For much of my childhood, I wrestled with an undiagnosed case of ADHD. I couldn't understand why I continually had trouble figuring things out, was easily distracted and often fell behind. I never understood the issue until I was in my thirties.

I struggled along most of the time. I never learned to think about, talk about, or discover who I was created to be. Yet, to speak to me, you would never know I struggled inside. I wore a smile no matter how I was feeling inwardly. I wore a smile no matter the circumstances. I wore a smile during those weekend trips back and forth from parent to parent.

As I grew up, my inward struggles started to show up on the outside too. I didn't know how to process the things that happened around me and to me. Many years would go by before I realized they happened "for me".

I kept most hurts inside me, safely tucked away, never to escape. That's what I observed those around me do. I'm here to tell you everyone needs to vent sometimes–yes, even you!

I know we can't rewrite the past, yet I've often wondered what it might have looked like had someone taken an interest in me. What if someone took the time to see my abilities, help me discover my learning style, and invested enough to see what was inside that wild, imaginative spirit? You know, crack the code on that kid. Now it's my pleasure to do this for others.

Oh well, since we can't go back, it is best to keep our focus on the windshield. After all, the review mirror is small for a reason.

We've all had moments of fear and uncertainty. We've all had times when it felt like nobody understood or cared.

I'm sure we've all been on the other side of that equation as well. We don't intentionally mean to "not care." Maybe we were too busy with those life issues that we forget to look around us, including those tiny people in our world or those younger than us. I certainly have.

Overlooked as a student, criticized and rejected as an adult and weakened as a wife. But I'm here to tell you while on this journey, I learned how to disregard those labels placed on me by others because I am in Christ. I'm an overcomer of my struggles and circumstances. Whether people intentionally meant to bring harm or not doesn't have to define me.

If you grew up in a home with both parents, peace, stability, full siblings, that is a gift. Count it as a blessing. Seriously!

If you're from a different home environment, be it a split home (like mine), foster homes, adopted parents, entirely on your own, or living with someone other than your biological family, the following is for you: Everyone has a story. Everyone goes through trials in life. It's what we choose to do with those trials that determine our destinies.

We often relate best to those who have been through the same thing we have. Sometimes those things weren't fun. I thank God for the life, parents, and situations He's given me, even though some of those not so enjoyable situations are still present in my life. I want to encourage you to be grateful too.

You might be wondering, "why should I be thankful?" Why should you be thankful and look for the good in your circumstances? Because the alternative is not God's best.

God has a plan for my life, just as He has a plan for your life. For me to fulfill my purpose, I had to go through some crap in life. Just like my parents did. Just like we all do.

Have you had some hard times? Don't be too hard on yourself, and don't be too hard on others. Everyone is just doing the best they can with the tools they have and with what they know at the time.

If someone doesn't know something, they don't know. Nobody sets out to be a bad person, become less than, homeless, lonely, or fearful in life. We all struggle, hurt, and go through valleys.

If that's where you are right now, know this, you're in good company. So come on, get up! Let's Go! God's mercies are new every day (Lamentations 3:22-23).

As we go through difficulties in life, we often get bombarded with people trying to offer unsolicited help. Ever experience this? Someone who means well, but they haven't been there, doesn't understand where you are, or maybe what God has planned for you.

If you're down in the sin pit (I like to call it) or just going through one of those "valley struggles" like depression or loneliness, please find someone you trust and confide in them. Find someone who has your best interest at heart, who can pray with you and give you a hand up.

When you're in line with God, yet are in a constant state of struggle, don't allow others to do your thinking for you. They'll create outcomes that seem right to them but are rarely best for you.

Don't live in fear or be overly concerned with what others expect out of you. Stop wasting significant amounts of time and energy, not being true to who you are. Meeting everyone else's expectations isn't God's best for you.

Keep asking God, even when it isn't clear. Figure it out. Then, stand up for what you believe.

I think it would be safe to assume everyone encounters fears of some sort regularly. Scripture gives us many verses on fear and reasons why we shouldn't live in it. It even instructs us not to allow it. Lessons on how to live fearlessly appear in the Bible so many times that we could apply one to each day of the year.

Suppose something is important enough to mention that many times, perhaps, we should spend some time on the subject. That brings me back to why fear is the subject I love. Well, it's His message about the topic of fear and His message of love. Fear and love abound at the core of every situation in life. There is no fear in love, but perfect love casts out fear (1 John 4:18).

If somebody told you, to win God's approval, you must act or be a certain way; I'm here to tell you that it just isn't so. They sold you a very misleading bill of goods. He loves you just as you are, unclean, broken, unlovable, unkind, uneducated, and unworthy. He loves you right where you are and just as much as He did before you were ever born.

You may feel like there is no hope for you or that you have made too many mistakes. Oh no, no, no–I guarantee I have made more, or maybe, we'll be in a close race.

God doesn't say get cleaned up first, and then I'll love you. He doesn't rescue us and says, "okay, you have three days, 7 hours, and 14 minutes to get this fixed, or you're out of here."

Did somebody tell you that you must do X, Y, and Z to be good enough to be loved by Him? It's not true.

His love is unlike anything you can imagine. He'll continue to pursue you regardless of where you are or what you've done, whether you want Him to or not, or even whether you're seeking Him or not. Now that's some genuine love, friends!

I can't tell you how often I got tangled in some awful stuff that was unpleasant to God. Yet, He pursued me over and over throughout the years. He never gave up on me.

What are the world's standards or your friend's standards? How about your parent's, family's or church's standards? By whose standards are we basing God's love, favor, mercy, and grace? I encourage you, DO NOT fall into this trap of protocol. If you do–RUN–run like heck to get away from it.

Be alert to the people or groups that trigger identity theft. They can mean well, but God doesn't have rules and regulations to be loved by Him. Once we accept the free gift of salvation, we do indeed have a responsibility. But somehow, somewhere along the way, many people got lost in someone else's opinion of their identity in Christ.

Remember, we're not all the same. Everyone's thumbprint is different, so how can someone else see, believe, and feel the exact perfect fit for me? They can't!

I use to believe that God was greatly disappointed in me and no matter how hard I tried He would always love someone else more and remain disappointed in me, until I learned to have a personal relationship with Him. Draw near to Him and see Him for yourself. Accept His free gift, His unconditional love, and then ask Him to lead you.

fearless growth®

"Grow with courage and confidence through
every experience life brings, facing fears head-on.
For with God, nothing shall be impossible."

– Becky Michel

I remember the day I realized I don't have to allow others to dictate, manipulate, or mold me into their system. It was not a gradual revelation; it was more like a jolt–Bam! God hit me with it hard, and all at once after ten years of living like everyone around me, not true to who I was. I call it my aha moment. It was both a very trying and freeing day.

God started me on my Fearless Growth® plan that day, and it continues more than ten years later. He gave me a calling, a vision, and a dream that day.

God can indeed use anybody where they are. He also has something more for us if we're willing to get out of our way and be patient enough to see it. That was me the day God announced He wanted to use me. He wanted me to stop people-pleasing and stand up to be the leader, and Becky, I was born to be. God asked me to share my story and instructed me on changes I needed to make. You see, I had become so good at putting aside my thoughts to take up everyone else's that I was not quite sure how to process such a big message from God that day.

I thought working on myself would take two or maybe three months tops. Boy, was I wrong! Seven years later–yes, you read that right– seven years later, before the story, God said I would share revealed itself. Why seven years? All the rejection and criticism, all the opposition I had to endure, overcome, push through are all part of my story I need to tell. God had been preparing through each leg of the journey.

Along the way, I would get off track, mess up, fall into the pit, or get myself into places I wasn't supposed to be. Yet, every time, God would pull me out of each mess up, problem, and wrong turn, and He would then prompt me to persevere. I repeatedly would try to throw the dream and vision down and give up. I even begged God to take it away, thinking it was too hard and heavy.

Changing myself, my relationships with others, and my way of thinking was not easy. God would continually pick me back up and tell me to keep going. Meanwhile, He was working, training me, and preparing others and their hearts so that one day, He would bring it all together in His perfect time.

Have you ever had to wait on God or felt as though He wasn't hearing you then come to find out He was making a way the whole time? I can't tell you how many times a random person would come up beside me—seemingly out of nowhere—and give me the nudge I needed to keep going. Angels among us?

Have you ever had something that just kept coming back to you again and again? Maybe, it's God nudging you? What's holding you back?

Fear inevitably brings denial, pride, arrogance, self-dependency, introversions, and bondage. It can trip us up when we deny the truth. I have seen time and time again people kept in bondage because they were afraid to face the truth or chose to live in a constant state of denial and face their giants head-on.

Ignoring something doesn't make it go away—it makes it worse. It may be uncomfortable, and it may get messier before it gets better. However, there is no victory over the situation until you get real.

Learn to conquer your denial battle. Reality brings humility. Humility allows us to tear down walls of fakeness.

Fear is a liar that holds us back. It causes a myriad of problems. If we live in denial, we'll never be able to embrace the life lessons found in our trials. It's through those situations we learn to grow. When we live in denial, we can't grow in the grace and knowledge of our Lord.

Don't dismiss your fears—face them. Clean up the messes you made and exercise your willpower to change directions. Then watch your life transform.

"Live to please God, not man." – *Becky Michel*

When you can't overcome your fear, know you have a God who can!

Use these scriptures to help you:

Fear thou not; for I am with thee: be not dismayed; for I am thy God: I will strengthen thee; yea, I will help thee; yea, I will uphold thee with the right hand of my righteousness. – Isaiah 41:10

There is no fear in love; but perfect love casteth out fear: because fear hath torment. He that feareth is not made perfect in love. – 1 John 4:18

The LORD is my light and my salvation; whom shall I fear? The LORD is the strength of my life; of whom shall I be afraid? – Psalms 27:1

What time I am afraid, I will trust in thee. In God I will praise his word, in God I have put my trust; I will not fear what flesh can do unto me. – Psalms 56:3-4

For ye have not received the spirit of bondage again to fear; but ye have received the Spirit of adoption, whereby we cry, Abba, Father. – Romans 8:15

Though an host should encamp against me, my heart shall not fear: though war should rise against me, in this will I be confident. – Psalms 27:3

Yea, though I walk through the valley of the shadow of death, I will fear no evil: for thou art with me; thy rod and thy staff they comfort me. – Psalms 23:4

Be strong and of a good courage, fear not, nor be afraid of them: for the LORD thy God, he it is that doth go with thee; he will not fail thee, nor forsake thee. – Deuteronomy 31:6

I sought the Lord, and he heard me, and delivered me from all my fears. – Psalms 34:4

facing giants with love

"Rather than denying fear, state it,
acknowledge it for what it is, then have
the courage to overcome it."

– Becky Michel

I had a childhood friend who would push, kick, and make fun of me in front of others to draw attention to herself, which she always seemed to accomplish. I would fight back tiny tears as the humiliation stripped away my self-confidence at my advancing age of–eight!

I don't think the age of offense matters so much as the effect it brings. Pain is pain, whether we are 8 or 88. Nobody likes a bully. Nobody wants to have their feelings messed with or have someone look down on them. Nobody likes to be the brunt of every joke, poked at, made fun of, hurt, used, or left standing in fear.

If you get nothing else from this book, please hear this–don't waste five more seconds on anybody who doesn't value you for who you are as a human. Don't bother with people who can't see past your imperfections and who don't love you for who you are despite your past, shortcomings, or differences. Please don't squander your energy on anyone who throws you under the bus or who only likes you for what you can do for them. That is not what love looks like; that is the territory where fear manifests.

People will come and go, in and out of your life, like a revolving door. They may be with you for a long time, or maybe just for a season. There's always a reason why if we allow God to show us. It's through those tough times and eye-opening moments that we're enabled to begin to experience Fearless Growth®.

Fearless Growth® only comes when we're willing to humble ourselves to receive and learn from these moments.

Let's go back to the woods. When the tree fell (aka your problem), you chose to acknowledge it and clear the path for not only yourself but also for anyone else who comes along the way. Why? Why does anyone do that? Because it was the right thing to do.

I still come across bullies. There will always be bullies. There will always be people who think more highly of themselves than they should, taking their issues out on others and try to feel better about themselves by putting others down. It's how we choose to respond to those individuals and situations that keep us stuck or drives us forward.

Bullies are like us. They are just people with pain, fear, and insecurities.

Note to self: Love covers a multitude...

The sooner you can forgive, the better. After all, forgiveness is for you.

Please don't put up with what God's already permitted you to free yourself from. No matter where you are, you can start over right now, right here. You can change. Heck, I'm not the same person I was a minute ago or even when I started this book. I'm free to start over now, free to be me, and free in Christ because today I know my identity in Him.

A life without growth is a life without purpose. Everyone, including you, was born on purpose, for a purpose, and with a purpose. Live your life on purpose every day. Living a life with purpose is my personal growth story–my Fearless Growth® journey.

Never say yes to others while saying no to yourself.

As I mentioned before, I was a dedicated people-pleaser. I was continually attempting not to upset the apple cart or rock the boat. I was at the side of every argument, bringing peace and love. I was trying to smooth over every conflict wherever they were. While some of this comes naturally because of who I am and how God created me, I used it the wrong way. I was never going to build confidence or feel peace living the people-pleaser life. I had embraced someone else's standard. It's no wonder we have such a mental health war among us.

Confidence and peace come once we see and correct those issues that we've allowed to control us. Whether that's people or actions, we do ourselves that we know we shouldn't be doing. And sometimes, those actions we should stop doing are good things.

We're not all here to carry out the same good deeds. God has different plans for each of us. Submit and align yourself with Him, and He'll show you if you should keep it or drop it.

Have you ever lived in an uneasy state? Insecure or afraid? This state is not God's best. As we have discussed before, we can't begin to experience Fearless Growth® until we face these issues head-on.

I've been in the most uncomfortable hot seat, more than once, I might add. It was hard to do, yet it was freeing when I did it.

It was like a jolt when I awoke to my spiritual blindness. Everyone's experiences are different. Your awakening will look different from mine, and we can all learn from each other. I'm here to walk alongside you just as God does for me so that you can see, understand, and overcome the areas that you're stuck. It may be one, three, or in all areas of life. Please know, there's always, always hope, and you can change. It's a power God gave you.

CHAPTER 6

courage
with heart

"Have courage and be kind. For where
there is kindness, there is goodness."

– Cinderella

Before we dive deeper into Fearless Growth®, I want to address the importance of having courage with heart. By heart, I mean a focused, driven conviction. It's a conviction that keeps you striving to be better, accomplish more, stretch, learn, and grow. It keeps you coming back day after day.

When we exhibit courage, we can push through life's challenges.

I knew a girl who made a lot of poor choices. It may have been because of her dysfunctional upbringing. Who doesn't have some dysfunction in their life, right? Was it based on her relationship with her parents? Her marriage wasn't quite the Cinderella story she had imagined it to be as a kid. Perhaps it was because of all those broken pieces or the fake love she suffered throughout her entire life? Maybe it had something to do with the inapt attention others gave her rather than nurturing her? Possibly it was the sense of feeling lost as most people experience from time to time throughout their lives.

Only God knows why she made the choices she did. Most likely, it was a combination of all the above. Choices affect our state, and our state dictates the roads we choose to go down. Our choices and our state go hand-in-hand.

If a person doesn't know to ask God to steer her ship, she doesn't know. If you're reading this and you've never read the Bible, and you're a Christian, (And, yes, that is possible. I know because I've been there.). How would you know to ask God to steer your ship if you haven't had biblical education? We don't know what we do not know. That has nothing to do with intelligence.

As a kid, I was a dreamer who watched a lot of TV shows. As you can see, I'm still quoting our beloved Cinderella. Well, everyone's life, as it turns out, isn't like it is in the movies. Fairytales don't always come true.

I think it's up to us to create our fairytale. A fairytale life comes from a grateful heart no matter your circumstances. It comes from noticing the good in times of trouble. It sees the best while at the bottom. It's lifting your eyes up to the hills when you're in the valleys.

Never give up on your dream. Never stop working towards it. Time and time again, I've seen people quit. I have seen them let their dreams go to the wayside.

Some dreams never come true due to various factors. It could be a lack of money, lack of time, or even lack of faith. It's possible, it just wasn't meant to be, or God closed the door for a reason. But know this, He never closes a door without opening another one, even when you don't recognize it. Dreams take faith and time.

Life is such a learning process. When we set out to do anything, it's always God's best for us to go at it with courage and heart. Let's face it; adversity will come. It's not if; it's when.

The power of positive thinking can focus you or refocus you. It can help you change your state. However, all the positivity you can muster will not get you the million dollars you need to fund that project or the farm you have big dreams of developing.

Zig Ziglar, a beloved mentor of mine and many others, had his first book rejected 39 times before he finally published it. That book published in 1974 is still in print today.

Look how many times Edison failed before he saw the light, no pun intended. Well, maybe a little. His teachers proclaimed he was too stupid to learn. He got fired from his first job. He made over 1,000 unsuccessful attempts at inventing the light bulb before success. Did he get frustrated at some point during that time? I guarantee it. Who wouldn't? Through all the adversity, how many times did he quit?

Courage with heart will not let you stop. You may say many times, "I quit." You might make changes or adjust the details, but you absolutely will not and cannot quit on your dream.

If you have something burning inside you, a dream you are dead set on, your courageous heart will not allow you to throw in the towel. Courage with heart is the driving force that sees you through to the end no matter what obstacles come your way.

Failure is just a stepping stone, an opportunity to try again. People told me "No" and criticized me countless times.

Courage with heart applies to all areas of life, not just a dream, including relationships, ventures, a mission, a job, skills, mindset, and more. It also applies to roles you may take on, such as a parent, teacher, or caregiver.

Have you ever been told you're wrong for pursuing your dream? You need to change or stop? No matter what you're up against, having courage, ignoring the "no's," and keeping the faith is a must.

Two little boys were playing near a well. The younger boy, age 7, felt down and discouraged about how much smaller he was than his friends. The older boy, age 8, suddenly fell in the well. The younger boy began to panic, not knowing what to do, because he first thought, as he always does, "I'm too small."

Notice, we become who and what we tell ourselves. The younger boy looked around for a solution. Seeing a bucket tied to a thick rope, he snatched it and threw it down the well. That little guy began the process of pulling his friend out all by himself.

In a time of crisis, this little boy found the courage and strength to do what he needed to do. Adrenalin kicks in during those crisis moments, but it's not adrenalin that shows you what you're capable of when put to the test.

There was no one around to discourage this little boy that he was too small or not smart enough to help. There was no one holding him back from rescuing his friend in that critical moment.

Think back to a situation where you just reacted. At that moment, you didn't focus on the negative self-talk you might typically have. You just did what was necessary.

We all have the power to be courageous, yet we must believe that we can. Believing is nurtured by turning down the dial on the critics and naysayers, setting healthy boundaries, and cutting ties with toxic relationships.

You must align yourself with Him, be willing to keep the faith and run with patience. It also means you stand up for what is right, even if that means standing alone.

It takes courage with heart to stand alone. If you don't take that stand, if you give up, if you quit, someone else will get the job done. God uses anyone, big, small, old, or young; it does not matter. He's just looking for someone willing to go for it. So, will you be a willing vessel? Will you choose to stay in the game regardless of the pain? Will you choose to have courage with heart?

For where there is kindness, there is goodness, and while not all of Cinderella's story is true to life, she showed kindness towards the unkindest, expecting nothing in return. That sounds a little like something Jesus would do. We won't always get it right. Yet, when we show kindness, even when someone wrongs us, we win.

I once read a quote, "Never regret being a good person to the wrong people. Your behavior says everything about you, and theirs says enough about them."

I love reading. I love how books push me to grow and challenge myself. I can't believe I just wrote those words! That was not always the case.

Years after my book report days had passed, I unknowingly discovered I love books. Once again, it was God who helped me find my book learning style and interest. He taught me how to thrive in areas where I was blind. Gosh, what would I do without Him?!

I love reading inspiring real-life stories about famous people, investors and the men and women behind the franchise and chain retailers Americans have grown to love. People from all walks of life, backgrounds, races, locations, including the US Founding Fathers, inspire me.

That's my interest. What books do you like to read? What inspires you or sparks your creativity?

Even when others hurt Cinderella, she found inner peace, saw the good in life, and kept a positive mindset. She possessed willingness and courage.

Now, if I disagree with someone, that doesn't mean they don't have anything good to say or that I can't learn from them. It simply means we have two different opinions or perspectives. That's okay.

It's also okay if you disagree with me. We're both entitled to our own opinion. We don't have to go to war. Like my aunt says, "Take what you can use and leave what you can't." Why does there have to be conflict over the rest?

Have you ever found yourself frustrated because someone didn't see it your way? Maybe, they were the ones getting irritated with you because you didn't see it their way. Most times, these are minor issues that aren't worth our time.

At the end of that interaction, you're probably distressed or have negative feelings, and you still don't see eye-to-eye. Ask yourself, "Was that exchange worth it?" "Did I just waste my time and emotional energy?" What is worth it is caring for yourself and nurturing your calling.

It takes courage to show up and be fully you. Regardless of what others want you to be, God's opinion is the only one that should concern you.

Part of courage with heart is developing grace under pressure; this helps you be gracious with others in trying times and demonstrate kindness in those pressure cooker moments.

And finally, be the person who faces and overcomes the challenges of life rather than running away from them. Please find a way around the fallen tree instead of high-tailing it out of the woods. When you do this, you'll look back and see that it was well worth it. You can say, "I ran my race–the race God had for me with courage."

the process of fearless growth® realness

"Never be afraid to be real
and shine those true colors."

– Becky Michel

1.   REAL - When I began to put Fearless Growth® together, I started with the one thing God wanted me to learn, which was to get real.

Being real doesn't mean I have to confess everything to everyone. It also doesn't mean I pick and choose what I want to see or change about myself.

Before you can experience salvation, you must see that you need God's forgiveness, mercy, and grace as a sinner. Before you can legally operate a car, you need a license. Before you can make an educated decision, you need the facts.

Before you can truly make changes, you must get down to the root issue. Digging down to the root issue begins with being real about who and where you are.

Transformation is possible. Surrendering to the struggle that keeps you at a standstill is necessary and essential.

Use the questions from the first chapter to help you get started. Then, delve into God's word and ask Him to reveal to you your core being, even those areas that are challenging. Remember, we shouldn't park in the past, yet we do have to address the issues that brought us here.

2.   THE GROWTH ZONE – The growth zone is where you decide to stay where you are or change.

If you fear change and remain at a standstill, you'll go in the opposite direction of growth. There is no stagnant area.

Growth is an uncomfortable feeling. You may feel oppressed or sad when you do not accept the challenge of growth. This challenge to yourself, or as in my case, a direct challenge from God, to learn who you are, become the best version of yourself, and step into what you were born for is not an easy task. Yet, it's a challenge worth taking when you're willing to do the work. You'll also become happier when you stop standing still.

You can sum up this book like this–GROWTH over FEAR.

Life is not about how much you know; it's about how much you grow.

Sometimes, losing is winning. Have you ever lost a few battles yet won the war? I certainly have. Those battles are often hard to choose.

Born to Win by Zig Ziglar, one of my all-time favorite books, taught me about a winning mindset. Sometimes, we lose to win. There are other times everything clicks, and we're on the same page with people. Those moments are sweet blessings from God. Yet, no matter what, look at every situation as an experience to grow. If you're growing, how can you not win?

3.   MINDSET SHIFT – Getting rid of what keeps us held back is not always easy. We say one thing and practice something different.

Ahh, the battles of the flesh. Mind shift starts with disciplining our minds.

If I say I'm lazy because that's what people told me or said to myself, I own that I'm indeed a lazy person.

Let's say you decided to begin the Fearless Growth® journey. You then wake up and say to yourself, "Who's lazy? Not me. I'm a hard worker," or you declare whatever it is you truly want to be. That does not mean–BAM–you instantly transform. Unless, of course, God sees fit to change you miraculously, there will be work involved.

During the growth process, I can either keep thinking the same thoughts, "I'm lazy, I can't do it, I'm worthless, I'm an alcoholic, I'm uneducated," and so on, or I can start implementing the mindset shift.

When you shift to positive words instead of those harmful, negative words, you'll feel the impact. I haven't arrived yet, but I'm living true to those new thoughts I think about myself.

It all starts in our minds. I think, therefore, I am. Scripture says, "I believe; therefore, I speak (2 Corinthians 4:13)." That is why it's okay to change your mind, to heed a conviction, God's calling, to better yourself and be more like Him.

Have you ever announced to your family or in a group how crazy you are, or maybe the fact you are always late, slow, dumb or such? I'm sure we all have, and do this from time to time, without thinking about those words, and while occasionally this is going to just naturally come out, it is good to be aware of our regular self-talk and behaviors then correct those that are negative when they start to become habits.

I have always smiled and laughed a lot, particularly because I like to have fun and be happy as much as I can. When I first joined Toastmasters, I learned that I would use a slight laugh as a crutch word or a filler for silence, mostly when I got nervous speaking or in a conversation. I began to work on this once I became aware of it. Not only was it annoying to me, but it showed a lack of confidence.

Can you believe that many of these same old habits will still try to sneak up from time to time even after I work on correcting them like the one, I just mentioned?

If I'm overweight and constantly announce that I'm fat, I'm claiming the promise to myself that I will stay fat! If I'm not overweight yet repeatedly say that I am, eventually, I will become those words. I have manifested it in my mind and to myself through my self-talk.

Now, if I'm comfortable in my skin, I might say, "I'm fat and sassy," or "I'm fat and happy." However, I don't recommend you do this repeatedly.

What we say about ourselves shows how we see ourselves. It reveals who we think we are.

Let's say I decide to go on a diet. Because of the words I've been speaking over myself, I'm to give up before I even get started. Our mindset makes all the difference.

A mindset shift is not going to come without work. Knowing your identity in Christ and who He says you are is vital to your mindset shift. You can employ a little "fake it till you make it" if needed as you're growing into your identity.

If you're having trouble believing your worth and value, I encourage you to test this out and see if it doesn't produce a healthy mindset shift. What you say to yourself, even if only in your mind, you start to believe. Then you eventually become what you say.

Confident, happy, clean, better, loved.

Don't believe me? Try it! Read Romans chapter 8.

Having the ability to get REAL begins in your mind.

You are a child of the King! Fearfully and wonderfully made, created by Him, forgiven, chosen, redeemed, wanted, and loved.

How are you not born to win with a mindset like that?

Did Jesus have the mindset of a winner? Look it up, and study for yourself. As I learned over the years, I've concluded that most personal growth and development are biblically based.

What's the alternative mindset to winning in life? What good does it do to carry that opposite thinking around?

Through Christ, I'm a winner, and because of that, I choose to win.

Now get up and get growing!

CHAPTER 8

no limits

"There is no fear in love…"

1 John 4:18

This chapter was so crucial that I made an entire book about it—Fearless Growth® – No Limits. When you learn to let go of limiting beliefs, that is when you begin to grow.

I didn't start with a plan all those years ago. I didn't have a life coach, although I became one soon after to help others, so they didn't have to go it alone. I didn't have anyone guiding me through a journey of personal development and self-discovery. I didn't know my next steps, how to implement them, or discover my purpose in life. It was just God and me.

This book is one way that you don't have to do this journey alone. You get the opportunity to learn from my mistakes and successes.

When we figure out who we are in Christ, as the scriptures say, we start to grow in grace and knowledge.

It was an interesting seven years chasing a dream God gave me, yet dang near everyone around me cut me down in some form or fashion. Through it all, I simply asked God to guide me. He was faithful even when my patience was gone. He was faithful even when I would veer off course. He was faithful even when I thought I couldn't take another step.

Life happened like it was supposed to. I can see that now. Why had I spent all those years earlier conforming to others' opinions, plans, and beliefs without realizing they were the very things that kept me in that state of feeling stuck and confused?

I just couldn't quite put my finger on it. I wasn't being true to who I really was and then living it. Your vision is clouded when you're looking through somebody else's lenses.

I learned who I am many years after my salvation experience, which came many years before I learned about being a Christian. I finally figured out my true identity many years after that.

God is so kind and gracious to us as we learn, mess it all up, try again, grow, and repeat. I'm incredibly thankful for His love, mercy, and grace.

During this time in my life, I learned that nobody could make me feel inferior without my consent. That was a profound statement for me, considering since, from the time I was eight years old, I believed everyone was against me. Why? Because some insecure, fluffy-haired little girl kicked me in front of the class and scarred me for life? There was a mindset shift and belief I created in that moment of hurt. We all do that, don't we?

Really! Take a minute and think back to a time when you were a kid. Can you see where somebody's opinion of you, or their mistreating of you, affected the way you saw yourself? Does it still affect you today?

Peoples' influence created our core personality and character traits at a very young age. Perhaps, you had people who positively influenced you, nurtured you and set you in a constructive direction. However, no matter the case, we create a story based on the people, and things around us at this young age and this is the story we tell ourselves as we grow, though good or bad.

I've studied the field of personal development for over a decade now. Why? Because personal growth & development was the element that was missing from my life. That's what God injected into me that day. Every person in the world needs personal development. It comes straight from scripture, just like Fearless Growth® does.

I fully believe that salvation is the foundation of life. Without it, we're like a structure that never reaches its greatest potential. We won't be able to withstand the wind and storms life brings us. Without salvation, we may have circumstances on our side, wealth, good looks, popularity, intelligence, and we're probably a great person. Still, without it, we're missing the solid foundation we could have, not to mention an eternal home in heaven.

It's hard enough to stand strong with Him. I struggle to imagine going through life alone. All the personal development in the world will not complete you. On its own, personal growth can't provide the peace that passes all understanding or freedom. I mean absolute, true freedom that can ONLY come from our Heavenly Father. Only then can you experience real growth, Fearless Growth®.

As I grew, I discovered I'd set my standards too high and was not open to change. Later I learned that a wise man does indeed change his or her mind many times!

I'd limited my belief system, limited my abilities, limited my relationship with God, His almightiness. Why? Fear. I wasn't aware I'd put limits on God, my faith, or myself–until that day.

It's fear that holds us back. It's fear that makes us unable to move forward in life. It's fear that hinders our growth.

Fear is like living in a box. God reached out His hand and helped me step out of the box I had put myself in.

Sounds pretty darn easy. Yea, not so much, but it's worth it a thousand times again.

We sure can mess it all up. The enemy has my number, and he's a pro at getting me off track. How about you?

Do you realize you can be a single parent, divorced multiple times, in a horrible place, miserable, beaten down, facing criminal charges, and God still loves you and can still use you? If you're willing, that is.

It's essential to learn to push through those limiting beliefs and fears. Pushing through fear can be a tool you practice in all areas of life, from convictions to addictions.

Let me introduce you to STOP N SWITCH®. It's a tool to help you shift your mindset from negative to positive thoughts. This tool makes it possible for you to overcome whatever roadblocks come your way.

STOP N SWITCH® is precisely what it sounds like. When your thoughts go in a negative direction, stop and switch to positive thoughts. You can't think a negative thought and a positive thought at the same time. You can also use this method with your actions. Just STOP N SWITCH® to make a change.

When you put this simple tool into practice, you become consciously aware. To be consciously aware means you can see yourself as you are, develop self-awareness, and practice self-examination regularly. People who are intentionally aware are honest, admit their faults, and see things for what they are, especially themselves.

perspective

"A life without growth is
a life without purpose."

– Becky Michel

Now that you are on the path to Fearless Growth® let's examine your perspective.

Life is all in how we see it. Our perspective is a key to unlocking Fearless Growth®.

Let me ask you, how well do you deal with life? You know, the stuff life throws at you?

Listen, fear exists. It's not going away. What matters is how we choose to view it and how we choose to deal with it.

Remember how we talked about the importance of our mental state? To keep a healthy mental state, we need to choose healthy ways to process fear.

Instead of excessively worrying about an issue, why not consciously practice an awareness tactic? Recognize you're "going there," and then choose to STOP N SWITCH®. Switch what you're thinking. Switch to a happy thought. Switch and call a friend instead.

You can also switch and choose to deal with an issue head-on instead of just sweeping it under the rug as though it doesn't exist (the proverbial elephant in the room).

That may sound intimidating, strange, or scary, yet when both parties are willing to be accountable and respectful of each other's feelings and opinions, it causes each person to grow.

We also need to take our focus off ourselves. Taking the focus off ourselves allows us to help others, which grants us the ability to see someone else's perspective.

Instead of being afraid of what someone thinks of you or what you think they feel about you, consider God's perspective. What does He say about you?

You can drive yourself crazy, focusing on what others think or don't think of you. It's not your job to control what someone else feels, thinks, or acts towards you. Your job is to take care of yourself.

When you need to shift your perspective, you can quote scripture, pray, help someone else, change your thoughts, or change your actions. Even going for a walk brings you back to a place of balance.

In scripture, David made several poor choices and suffered the consequences, yet he didn't let his mistakes stop him. God even said David was a man after His own heart.

Never allow the troubles you come up against slow you down or hold you back. Remember, you're unique, intelligent, and highly gifted!

Please don't allow anyone to convince you to do something simply because it's to their advantage, gain, glory, or help them feel better about themselves. If this is the kind of people you're hanging with, it's time to cut some ties and expand your circle of influence.

There are times in life we must let people go!

What about the people who continually get upset with you? While these people probably don't intentionally mean harm, they're not a friend! They might be great people who mean well, and it's okay to let them go.

God permits us to let His people go when it is time; He will show you.

Setting boundaries is one of the best things you can do for yourself. It's also the kindest thing you can do for yourself and them. You don't need anyone's permission; you have God's.

God has given you wisdom, and it's okay to have opinions. So, don't spend time listening to what everyone else wants you to do when you can hear God for your situation. Listen for His peace.

You may believe you need these people, but you don't. In the Bible, God whittled down Gideon's army from 32,000 to 300, and God used the 300 to bring a tremendous victory over a multi-nation army that was so large the Bible said their army was "thick as locusts."

I realize you displease others to please God. You must be secure enough to say, "I am not a people pleaser; I am a God pleaser." I believe fearing people should be dealt with immediately.

Also, don't allow anyone to make you feel guilty for being yourself. While these people in my life may have meant well, I would find myself listening to what they told me. That caused me to wrestle with what God specifically told me to do. Perhaps it was what God showed them to do, yet it wasn't suitable for me.

Over the years, when I tried to follow what someone else told me I should do, I realized it didn't line up with what God put in my heart and the direction He was leading me.

Sometimes people don't hear God for you, which is why it's essential to focus on what God told you and run your race. Like the Apostle, Paul told us, "I am not seeking to win the approval of people but of God."

If they leave you, it's okay; let them go. A well-meaning person may try and hold you back; be strong, be bold, and follow God.

When you fear standing alone, give it to God immediately. Again, never be afraid to stand up for what is right. Adversity distracts and clouds your perspective.

Our enemy, Satan, may try to get us questioning our race, the purpose God gave us. He does this through good things and great people. For example, God called my friend to one area, and He called me in a different direction. Satan can quickly and easily have me questioning what I'm doing. I can see the fantastic things she is doing, or she may make suggestions for me. It doesn't take long before I'm off track from what God called me to do. Even Jesus had to say to His disciple Peter, "Get behind me, Satan," when Peter inadvertently tried to distract Jesus from His calling.

The enemy will use anything to distract you and get you off track, even use our brothers and sisters in Christ.

We must stand up for what God has shown us. We each have our race to run, and we can still learn from one another.

You'll never become or accomplish all you are born to if you must have the approval of others. Our God-given job is to love God first, then love one another just as they are, not for who we want them to become. God didn't give us the job to change, shame, or manipulate others into our vision of who they should be. It's our job to love others where they are.

Learn to look at others through God's lens–love. When you understand how loved you are, you will experience profound change, and you will be free to love others unconditionally. Understanding God's love for us is the heartbeat of Fearless Growth®.

Now, what do we do with criticism when it comes? First, examine it to see if you can learn from it. When we can take constructive criticism with humility, we grow.

Often, when people criticize us, we get defensive. However, criticism can be our friend if we allow it.

Whether you're young or old, it's imperative to be humble enough to change when we need to. Learn to ask questions when you don't know the answers and don't feel ashamed about it.

Stand up for what you believe, yet be humble enough to hear what others are saying. Then examine yourself to see if you need to listen to their advice, change or grow. Perhaps, they're God's messengers.

If, after testing their criticism, you feel they don't have your best interest at heart, don't waste your time holding onto that negative feedback.

However, if you've examined them and found they have your best interest at heart, find a middle ground. Scripture says, "Great peace have they which love thy law and nothing shall offend them."

By the way, how is your love walk?

Do you demonstrate love, compassion, and service when dealing with people, even the difficult ones? How do you handle it when someone has a different way of doing things than you do? Are you able to respond in love, or do you react?

When you respond, you practice love and compassion for the other person and in service to God.

There may be times you have to take a deep breath, or two, walk around the block, or in my case, the barn, or even scream in the car before you can respond correctly. That's okay. Do it.

When we react, it's a defense mechanism that happens without us thinking about it. Reacting is acting in the "Flesh." Nothing good comes when we react. Trust me, I know. I've taken many walks around the barn or "losing it" in the car to avoid reacting all over someone else.

I don't get it right every time. I've reacted enough for ten people's lifetimes. Even though God has taught me what I'm sharing with you, I still live in the flesh, so there's that.

CHAPTER 10
the right time

"Although my path may look
different, and I may sometimes
seem to wander, I am not lost."

– Becky Michel

Have you ever felt like God gave up on you? Have you thought, "Where are you, God?"

If you know me or have ever heard me speak, you know that I'm big on being real and laying it out there. My first pastor, who was an extraordinary person in my life, called getting real "shelling the corn."

We may as well be honest; God knows anyway, right?!

So, here's me getting real. It was tough for me to finish this book series. I started writing over five years ago, but the words would never come. No matter how hard I tried or how much I prayed, it just wasn't working.

Picture trying to put together a jigsaw puzzle using identical pieces. It may have been the hyper-focus superpower of my ADHD kicking in, but the writing process was exhausting. It was a horrific experience, and it mentally and emotionally drained me. I cried out to God, "You wanted me to do this, so why isn't it working?"

Today, I understand–it wasn't the right time–yet. There was more I needed to learn and grow through. God gave me the name 'Fearless Growth®' at the beginning of the COVID pandemic. I'd been coaching pieces of this process for years but could never come up with the title until that moment. I had to wait. Did I mention I do not like to wait?

Waiting on God has been one of the hardest things I've done in my life. He has revealed to me, time and time again, why it's crucial to wait even when it is hard and not so fun. He also taught me some tough lessons about trying to get ahead of His timing. Those lessons were even less fun.

I've sat in the "waiting room" many times in life. Sometimes with a good attitude, and other times impatiently pacing. Did I mention I don't have much patience?

Ever been to the school of hard knocks? I'm working on my second doctorate there! I've gained an irreplaceable education in that school. I'd never trade my street smarts and the growth I experienced through the many challenges for a college education. It's okay if you disagree. It's my book–my story.

Some of the most extraordinary people have done some of the most amazing things with limited resources, without college, heck without a sixth-grade education. Some were from a small town, poverty-stricken, rejected, or disabled, or what I like to call superpowers of those with special needs.

Ever hear of Johnny, the bagger? He was a grocery store bag boy with down syndrome. With a simple yet grand act of kindness, he impacted the lives of countless people in his town.

Johnny began to put a 'thought for the day' in every bag of groceries he bagged. People came to that store to stand in Johnny's line. That signature gesture made him one of the most loved grocery baggers of all time.

Those with special needs inspire me every day to never give up, run my race, and live my purpose!

Do you allow your challenges to be a crutch or a handicap? They can camouflage themselves as excuses. Johnny didn't. Even though he had down syndrome, he wanted to work. Zacchaeus was small, yet he made a way to see Jesus by climbing a tree.

Where there is a will, there is a way. It all starts with the right mindset. "I can't" limits you. "I can" empowers you. I'm too big, too small, too broke, too old, too whatever–the truth is your too afraid! It's the fear that's limiting you.

The excuses are lies from the enemy to keep you right where he likes you, beaten down and stuck. It's your choice to use those excuses or not.

When we move in the direction God wants us to take the necessary steps to change and transform, God is faithful. It doesn't matter how long it takes. Please, keep in mind, some lessons take you longer to learn. That's been the case for me anyway. He's still faithful.

I learned one of these lessons a few years ago while coaching on confidence. I wrote a book, but not the book I was supposed to. I remember being so uneasy even to have it proofed. I understand now why I wasn't supposed to publish that book. Through this lesson, I gained a deeper understanding of my struggle with impatience–the wait.

The journey can be joyous and the process priceless if we'll simply learn to embrace the moments and step into them, being present, learning, loving, laughing, and enjoying, even those hard lessons. I mean, what's the alternative?

CHAPTER 11

failing forward

"Fall quickly, getting right back up.

Fall often, in order to learn from your mistakes,

but always fall forward, to never stop growing."

– Becky Michel

Last year I went ziplining for the first time with my sisters. Had I known there was a hundred-foot jump at the end I would have most likely opted out. Now mind you, this is from the girl that always wanted to skydive. Bungee jumping has always scared me, and while it's not "technically" bungee jumping, it's close. As we came down to the last platform I looked around, starting to sweat with fear. "Where is the last zip that takes us to the ground?" I asked. The girl stationed at this platform said "that was it, you just put your feet on the edge and jump off now". As I looked down a hundred feet at a small circle in the woods, all I could think was I am lunging to my death, today's the day. As I stood with my toes on the edge wondering if this harness would catch me, I turned around to my sister and said "you're going to have to push me." I panicked as I thought of an alternative way to get down, shimmy down the pole, maybe pull myself back up the line, anything but jump. Within a few short minutes, I eventually made that jump and amazingly the harness caught me at the thirty-foot mark and hoist me to a soft landing. I share this to say as we come up against the world and all the difficult things we don't always want to do, continue to fail forward, even if you must ask your sister to push you now and again!

I challenge you to run your race without apology, to dream big, and to stay in the game regardless of the pain and always being true to yourself.

One of the saddest statistics documented is that people reveal they regret not being true to themselves in the last hours of life. They wished they cared less about what others thought of them. They lamented living in fear instead of living their life full-out.

Many have said, "I wish I'd dared to live a life true to myself, not the life others expected of me," "Why did I work so much," or "I should've had the courage to express my feelings."

I'm on a full-blown mission to change that statistic!

Has God given you something to do, a message to share, or somewhere to be? Just go! Just do it! Get started today–right now.

Please don't wait until it's too late. Make changes, grow, and pray. Choose to be free from the fears holding you back. Start now and live true to who God's called you to be.

If I hadn't started when God spoke to me, hung in there throughout so much negativity and did my self-work, I wouldn't be writing this book that has taken me for-e-v-e-r.

Had I flat out said no or drug my feet because the assignment appeared too big, I would have grown–zero, most likely divorced, and you wouldn't be reading what God gave me to share. Oh, not to mention the depression I would experience that comes with regret. I know this because I've done a lot of self-medicating and poor habit practicing to soothe my frustrations, pain, etc. Yes, all of this happened even while walking with God. The flesh is weak!

What if I would have listened to others? What if I'd allowed the problems and the struggles, I encountered to keep me down? What if I just gave up?

After seven years, I've exclaimed, "Lord, how much longer am I going to have to wait?" Could I have made some better choices that got me there sooner? More than likely, yes. Did God want me there sooner?

Only He knows. What good would it do me to spend time wondering now? You're right. It wouldn't do me any good. So, I continually move forward.

I'm unashamed, even with a past full of mess-ups, regrets, fears, and challenges. I've learned to grow fearlessly. I'm free to be myself and express my God-given opinions, ideas, and creativity.

You have incredible gifts and talents. People need what you have. My prayer is that you'll join me on a journey of Fearless Growth® to do the same.

God's light and love heal wounds. When we flee from sin, align with Him and learn to live life, not just be alive, life becomes free and complete.

I was a broken vessel with tons of mistakes under my belt, yet I was a willing vessel who said yes–yes to Fearless Growth®. How about you?

We're all vessels. However, willingness is a choice. Choosing humility or pride is a deciding factor in our most significant, most fearful, dreaded choices.

I'm where God wants me. I'm confident in Him and in who I am. Yes, I have made a truckload of mistakes, yet I'm willing to be humble enough to acknowledge the errors, face the consequences, and persevere.

God gave me this story. What does God have for you? It's different for all of us.

Never forget that love is always the key when dealing with people. That is the lens God desires you to view others through.

Stand up for yourself and what you believe. Have conviction and heart to run your race. Transformation begins with surrender. What do you need to surrender so you can start your Fearless Growth® journey today?

CHAPTER 12

stand

"Sometimes it takes a good fall
to really know where you stand."

– Hayley Williams

Have you ever found yourself just existing in life, bored, down, discouraged, feeling like there's got to be more to it all than this? That was me, living life thinking, is there more for me and if so what and where is it? I had just finished lunch and was sitting across the table from my husband with a group of friends when one of them quietly said to me "it pleases me to see you serving your husband better", that was it! A significant moment for me where God spoke that this is not His best for anyone. Not me, not the person instructing me and checking to see if I followed the instruction, not the person I am serving in the cunning bitter way of which I was doing it, nobody was benefitting in this situation. Remember earlier when I said every relationship should have mutual respect? My marriage did not have that at the time this took place and this was a turning point for me. I knew that no matter what else there was in my future, I was not okay with what and how I was being as a wife, and no matter what, I would not continue allowing anyone to make me feel this way, especially myself. For the first time I realized what an identity struggle I was in.

I'll never forget that day when God answered my question, "What is my purpose?" This was just a glimpse of much heartache and frustration I had to walk through to get that answer. He called me to inspire others who struggled in the same areas I have.

Talk about scary and exciting all wrapped up together!

When I began to share my story with a handful of people, all the negative nellies came out of the woodwork to make sure I knew this was a stupid idea.

"You're going to tell people what? Like a little story?" "Oh, you think you can write a book? Wait, didn't you flunk English?" "You're going to speak, like a motivational speaker?"

Read those last few sentences over again, but now with an indignant gaze and in a snarly, arrogant voice. That's it! That is exactly how it sounded when I heard it the first time…ha-ha.

People criticized me not just one or five times, but I'm talking countless times. I experienced rude and cynical people, harsh statements, and an unbelievable amount of disapproval. I faced tons of naysayers and money-hungry Christian companies with no regard for my mission to accomplish what God had called me to do.

This wasn't just a Becky dream; this was a God dream. It was a God dream with tons of rejection. "No, I won't help you," "No, I'm not giving you any advice," and "No, you can't work with me."

Someone even plagiarized one of my children's books. Geez, I was just on a mission to simply run the race God gave me while trying to figure life out like everyone else.

Now, everyone didn't treat me this way. Many tremendous people have helped me over the years, but, sadly, it was less than I'd hoped.

The truth is that life can be tricky, confusing, and dang hard sometimes. Doing anything of significance in life can come with people who won't understand you. The judgers may come out to the party, whether you invited them or not. They came out to my party like a pack of dogs on a three-legged cat.

During this time, God showed me how to connect with scripture and apply it personally, which I desperately needed. I also learned to keep it to myself, like Mary, the mother of Jesus, did as she pondered these things in her heart. I realized that not everyone is going to understand my purpose. Know too that not everyone will understand your dreams either.

WHEN YOUR CHANGING YOURSELF IT
GETS LONELY, BUT CHOOSE GROWTH
OVER COMPANY!

BECKYMICHEL.COM

I felt so lonely chasing that dream God gave me all those years ago. However, I learned so much during that time. God taught me I needed to let go of certain relationships, and I developed the ability to stand up for myself. I discovered how to be more positive and how to stop people-pleasing. I uncovered who I was created to be, solidified what I believed, and finally understood what made me, me–Becky. I also began my entrepreneurial journey.

As I reflect, I realize the challenges I went through taught me specific tools that continually help me grow. I'm living proof that if you hang in there and keep going, our God will never fail you.

It was a rough ride and hard to hang on, but looking back, I see God's hand throughout the entire process.

At one time, I was part of a network marketing company. I did a ton of cold calls, you know, the dreaded calls to people who have no idea who you are. I also made countless calls to people that personally knew me. No one enjoys getting hung up on hundreds of times.

I can laugh today because I see the lessons that life hammered into me. One of those lessons was how to handle rejection. I know I'm not alone in this experience.

Today, as I continue to grow myself, I'm privileged to work with thousands in their personal growth and development journey. Through this, I can see we're all in a different place in our journey.

Our journey is like a ladder. It has many steps to it. That's why we need to have patience and love to endure others who may not be where we are.

My mentor told me, "You are not as good as you are going to be, but you are better than you once were, and you are good enough for where you are at the moment."

I now see how this applies to our life journey. I know for myself there are times I've had to stay on a step of that ladder longer than I want to. That's where I learned patience. Wait, did I mention patience was not my thing?

Thank God for His mercy! I'll never please everyone. As someone once said, "You can please some of the people all of the time. You can please all of the people some of the time, but you will never please all of the people all of the time." That's a good thing to know. I don't have a desire, or the energy, to be a people pleaser anymore.

I learned to face fears and rejection from my own family and close friends. An arduous process, but I needed this process so God could position me where He wanted me.

Today, I work with other leaders in various areas and ministries. With God, I do many things people don't understand or define as weird. I teach people to dream big and live unashamed regardless of their past. Since God forgave you—that's it! The devil is the one trying to shame you with your past. Do not accept the shame.

I accepted God's plan for my life, which, by the way, was not the direction I would have steered the ship. I tried "steering the ship" a few times; that was a bad idea. When I surrendered my need to control the direction, my journey became more effortless.

Transformation is possible. Surrender is required.

Two paths diverged in the woods, and I took the one less traveled, and that has made all the difference.

When you come to the end of your race, will you be able to say I did the best I could? I made mistakes, yet I was true to myself, and I was the person God created me to be? If not, my prayer for you is that you'll choose to take that journey.

If you see me around, remind me of that too, because He's still working on me every day. I don't always get it right; I don't always grow, say the right thing, or take the needed actions. I'm not always the best mom or wife. I battle the flesh like you. Aren't we all on this journey of life together?

CHAPTER 13
unashamed

"Be real and unashamed, even of
your mistakes and faults."

– Becky Michel

As I wrap up this glimpse into my life, the story of a wandering people pleaser, I leave you with the best advice God gave me– EXAMINATION.

Examination brought me to my core and revealed my true self like nothing else.

Examine yourself, not just today, but daily. Examine yourself not just a little; examine yourself a lot!

You can start with these questions:

- What is the one thing standing between me and the real me?

- What are my fears? Am I willing and ready to face them?

- Am I a people pleaser?

- Am I prepared to experience growth?

If you're a people pleaser, I challenge you to muster the courage to change. People-pleasing isn't God's best for anyone. People pleasers never make an impact.

When you conform to what others want, you often get into trouble. I know; I've been there too.

Have you ever tried to fit a round shape into a square hole? You might eventually shove it into the hole, but it doesn't fit correctly, and you most likely will damage it in the process.

There will be times in your life you don't have anyone to lean on or have anyone willing to guide you. There will also be times no one is around to encourage you or run alongside you. What will you choose to do then? What will you do when you feel alone?

Just like you, there have been times I had no one; not even my husband could help me. That's no offense to him; we were growing in different directions at that time in our marriage. That was some of our marital growing pains at the time.

Standing up for something you believe in takes a lot of courage. It may require standing alone. A key to standing alone is to learn to encourage yourself, just as David in the Psalms did. Learning to encourage myself got me through almost impossible, yet very significant, times in my life.

No one else is going to do it for you. Staying in the same place means you're moving backward. How may you ask? If you aren't moving forward, you're stagnant. If you're stagnant, you'll eventually begin moving in the wrong direction. Trust me; it happens every time. Just like allowing someone to bring you down to where they are, if you stay passive, it won't take long before you go backward again, and boy does relapse suck! Growth is vital to conquering the fears that keep you stagnant, and it comes through continually moving forward.

You may be going through a trial right now. I don't know why you're reading this book. Maybe someone gave it to you, or you met me somewhere and wanted to see what Becky Michel is all about. Perhaps, the title intrigued you.

Hopefully, you see me as a Jesus lover, wife, mom, hope dealer, and inspirer. I also love being inspired. I love the farm life, my family, trying new things, and helping amazing people like you grow into who God created them to be. I love pursuing my calling of Fearless Growth®. I love showing others how to live it, how to stand up for themselves, how to stop people-pleasing and how to find their purpose. It's my passion to help people discover who they truly are and experience peace and freedom in that.

You can know Christ and wander through life like a lost feather in the wind. I was there, standing in those woods facing that fallen tree once upon a time.

As we journey through life making choices, facing difficulties, experiencing failures, and pushing through struggles, we all discover the common denominator—fear.

You may not have realized it was fear blocking you until now. Fear is a master conman. It loves to disguise itself as excuses. It especially loves to distract us from the truth. Its specialty is keeping us from fulfilling our purpose.

What do you fear?

I sought the Lord, and He heard me and delivered me from my fears.

God's word tells you not to be afraid because He is with you. He instructs you to be strong and of good courage. He is with you when you stand up to your giants. He picks you up when you get knocked down. He reminds you of who you are when you struggle to see your true self.

I will leave you with this—be the fearless, authentic version of yourself, willing to face fear head-on. Learning to overcome Shame, Fear, and Limits!

Much Love, Becky

Becky Michel

Transformation is Possible   Surrender is Required

BeckyMichel.com

Becky runs the Fearless Growth® Program based on her message of becoming the person God created you to be as you push through the fears that hold you back from becoming your best YOU. Live a life of purpose, on purpose, for a purpose! The 3-part program is for those who wish to learn personal transformation through Fearless Growth®. PM or contact her for more details or to sign up for her elite workshop.

Get Real, Get Rid, and Get Going – An eBook
An introduction to Fearless Growth®, now available on Amazon.

Becky captures your audience with customized workshops, with workbooks, Bible studies, and study guides, tailored to fit your event while adding her message of Fearless Growth®.

You've just completed Volume 2 -No Fear, as you've gotten to know Becky and her struggle with fear, people-pleasing, and learning to be who God wanted her to become through overcoming life's challenges.

Check out the other two volumes to continue the three-step process of Fearless Growth®.

Volume 1, No Shame–Ignite your purpose with Fearless Growth®. No Shame is the first book in the Fearless Growth® series. Discover how to overcome the shame that holds you back so you can live the Fearless Growth® life that God is calling you to live.

Volume 3, No Limits–Pursue the Power of Fearless Growth®. No Limits is the last volume in the Fearless Growth® series. Now that you're learning to live fearlessly explore life with no limits through Fearless Growth®.

To book Becky for speaking, find her at Beckymichel.com / 417-293-5340 / Becky@BeckyMichel.com

There is no fear in love, but perfect love casts out fear because perfect love banishes all fear. If we are afraid, it is for fear of punishment, and this simply shows that we have not fully experienced His perfect love. The only fear we should grant permission is that which is in reverence and respect to God. Thou shalt fear the Lord thy God and serve Him. Work out your own salvation with fear and trembling. Love still abounds at the root of this. We should desire to be and do good because we love God.

Bonus Section:

"I like to think of a Dream Board as a growth guide!"

Dream Board in 3 Easy Steps

Items Needed:

- Post It's and a sharpie
- A paper to lay/draw it out before you start (optional)
- Craft supplies: glue, paint, markers, pens, poster board, magazines, or a Pinterest account and program to paste pictures if going the digital route.

Step 1 – Brainstorm

It's BRAINSTORMING TIME! Don't be afraid to DREAM BIG! Get your post-its out now! You can use a sheet of paper if you'd rather.

You can live the life you live now and love. I encourage you to find joy.

Incorporate the Fearless Growth® life you want.

- Write down everything want that comes to your mind.
- One dream per each post-it!
- I create a new dream board for EACH YEAR.
- Don't be afraid to put now-and-then pieces of your life as well as time-sensitive items.
- Be sure to incorporate the seven Joy Flow areas listed on page 89.

Here Are Questions to Help You Brainstorm:

- Sometimes I do a possibilities and realities section to show a list of things I've accomplished or change each year.
- What are your interests?
- What do you like? What brings you Joy? These can be simple and BIG!
- What are your passions?
- Likes, Feels, Tastes?
- What do you like to do for fun?
- Describe your ultimate day?
- Where are you going?
- What type of person do you want to be?
- What type/style do you want your life to be?
- What changes do you want to make/add to your life?
- Do you want to change your lifestyle? What represents that?
- Where places would you like to visit or explore?
- List any needs you have, like "braces for the kids," vehicles, etc.

- What have you always wanted to accomplish?
- Do you have unfinished projects you want to complete?
- Do you have a word for the year?
- Who is important to you?
- What is your life mantra?
- What specific goals are you accomplishing this year?
- What is the result of what you want to happen this year?
- What are your marriage or relationship goals?

Step 2 – Set Goals

Setting goals is crucial for this project.

You can use the SHARP method of goal setting listed below or use another goal-setting method.

Do make sure whatever method you choose uses specific targets.

Targets help overcome triggers, move forward, and help you accomplish your goals on time.

Goals are how YOUR dreams are born!

SHARP GOAL SETTING TOOL

S	**SPECIFIED:**
	Write exactly what it is you wish to accomplish in detail.
H	**HELP MYSELF & MEASURE MINI:**
	Use smaller mini-goals to measure progress based on what works for you.
A	**ATTAINABLE:**
	Make your goal ambitious, yet not outrageous; it should be realistic.
R	**REASONABLE:**
	Make sure the goal is reasonable for your season of life. Not over complex.
P	**PROMPT:**
	Promptly get busy. Give yourself time and set a deadline.

Step 3 – Decide on a Style

Now that you have your goals set, you want to pick the style dream board you wish to create.

Here are a few ideas:

- If going digital, use Pinterest to create a digital board. Simply pin what you want to use. Pinning saves the pictures.

- You can open each pin once you have your board made and screenshot them or save the images to your computer; keep the pictures in a specified folder.

- Next, print the photos and put them on your poster board, around your desk, on a wall, or even copy and paste into a Word doc and pin to your PC screen; share with yourself.

- You can use canva.com or picmonkey.com to make a digital board or use Shutterfly to create a book.

- Your dream board can be an entire wall, multiple small frames, one board on the back of a door, or a simple poster board.

Do whatever floats your adventure boat! Get creative! Creating is the fun part!

Dream Board Style Ideas:

THE JOY FLOW AREAS
TO CONSIDER:

The Joy Flow wheel consists of areas of life to consider when developing dreams and goals. When we can maintain a balance that flows in these seven areas of life, we can begin to experience fulfillment and joy!

1.SPIRITUAL   *2.MENTAL*

3.FINANCIAL   *4.PHYSICAL*

5.FAMILY   *6.CAREER*

7.PERSONAL

CPSIA information can be obtained
at www.ICGtesting.com
Printed in the USA
BVHW091325030322
630567BV00007B/272